MY FIRST LOOK

AT PLANETS

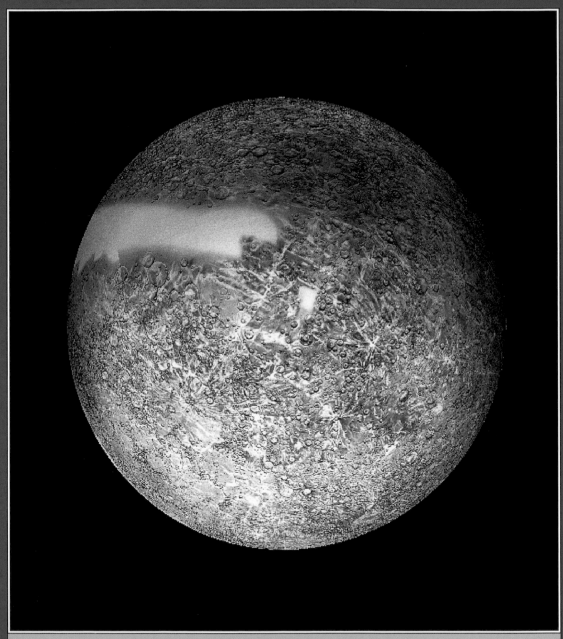

THE SURFACE OF MERCURY IS VERY ROUGH

Mercury

TERESA WIMMER

CREATIVE EDUCATION

Published by Creative Education

P.O. Box 227, Mankato, Minnesota 56002

Creative Education is an imprint of The Creative Company

Designed by Rita Marshall

Photographs by Bridgeman Art Library, Photo Researchers (Chris Butler / Science Photo Library, A. Gragera / Latin Stock / Science Photo Library, Ludek Pesek / Science Photo Library, Science Photo Library, U.S. Geographical Survey / Science Photo Library, Detlev Van Ravenswaay / Science Photo Library), Tom Stack & Associates (Brian Parker, TSADO / NASA)

Copyright © 2008 Creative Education

Printed in the United States of America

Library of Congress Cataloging-in-Publication Data

Wimmer, Teresa, 1975- Mercury / by Teresa Wimmer.

p. cm. — (My first look at planets)

Includes index.

ISBN-13: 978-1-58341-519-1

I. Mercury (Planet)—Juvenile literature. I. Title.

QB611.W56 2007   523.41—dc22   2006018249

First edition 9 8 7 6 5 4 3 2 1

MERCURY

Near the Sun

A long time ago, people looked up in the sky. They saw a small, bright dot that looked like a star. But the dot was not a star. It was the **planet** Mercury.

Mercury is part of the **solar system**. Besides Mercury, the solar system has seven other planets. All of the planets move in an **orbit** around the sun. Mercury is the closest plan-et to the sun.

THE SUN LOOKS VERY BRIGHT FROM MERCURY

Mercury spins like a top in the sky. It never stops spinning. But it spins very slowly. One day on Mercury lasts for more than 1,000 hours. That would mean a very long day at school!

Still and Quiet

Up close, Mercury looks like a gray, bumpy ball of rock. It is covered with **craters**. Mountains and flat lands called plains cover Mercury's ground.

A long time ago, Mercury
used to be bigger. It slowly
shrank over many years.

MERCURY'S CENTER MAY BE MADE OF IRON

Nothing moves on Mercury. There are no clouds. There is no wind. There is no rain or water, either. No people or animals live on Mercury. There are no trees or flowers. The sky is black instead of blue.

Mercury has no moons. From Mercury, the sun is the biggest thing in the sky. It looks like a huge, bright ball in Mercury's black sky.

From space, Mercury looks very
bright. Light from the sun
bounces off it and makes it shine.

MERCURY SHINES BRIGHTER THAN SOME STARS

Hot and Cold

Only half of Mercury faces the sun at a time. The half that faces the sun has daytime. During the daytime, the air is hotter than fire. The half that is turned away from the sun has nighttime. During the nighttime, the air is colder than ice.

The top and bottom of Mercury are called the poles. Mercury's poles have ice on them.

Planets and stars are different.
Stars stay in one place. But
planets are always moving.

METEORITES, OR FALLING ROCKS, ONCE HIT MERCURY

Shadows from the craters help to keep the ice from melting.

Mercury has almost no fresh air. The sun gives off a strong, hot wind. A long time ago, the sun's winds blew most of Mercury's air away.

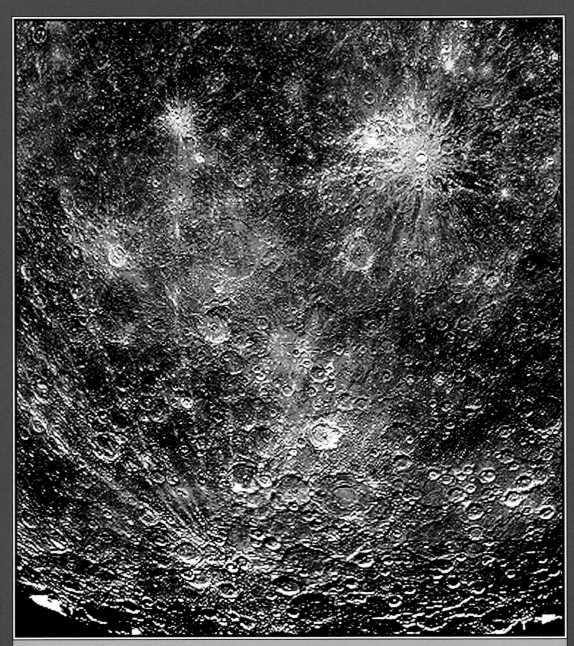

SOME OF MERCURY'S CRATERS ARE MANY MILES ACROSS

More to Learn

People still do not know a lot about Mercury. What they do know, they learned from pictures. The pictures were taken by **probes** sent to Mercury.

The probes were very strong so that they would not melt in the sun's heat. They took many pictures of Mercury. But the probes only got close enough to see some of the planet.

Mercury spins slowly, but it
moves very fast around the sun.
That is because it has a short trip.

MERCURY IS NEAR THE CENTER OF THE SOLAR SYSTEM

A few years ago, another probe took off for Mercury. It will take seven years to get there! The probe will circle Mercury for a long time. It will take many new pictures of Mercury. From the pictures, people hope to learn more about Mercury!

PROBES FIRST VISITED MERCURY ABOUT 30 YEARS AGO

Hands-on: Make a Planet Mercury

Mercury is a very bumpy planet. You can make your own planet Mercury and watch it spin!

What You Need

A small Styrofoam ball

A piece of yarn about eight
   inches (20 cm) long

A gray marker

A pencil with an eraser

Glue

What You Do

1. Color the Styrofoam ball gray.
2. Use the eraser end of the pencil to make small dents all over the ball.
3. Glue one end of the yarn to the top of the ball.
4. Now you have your own planet Mercury. Hold on to the top of the yarn. Make Mercury spin!

MERCURY'S SURFACE IS UNLIKE ANY OTHER PLANET'S

Index

Words to Know

craters—big holes in the ground made when something crashes into a planet

orbit—the path a planet takes around the sun or a moon takes around a planet

planet—a round object that moves around the sun

probes—special machines that fly around or land on a planet or a moon

solar system—the sun, the planets, and their moons

Read More

Rudy, Lisa Jo. *Planets!* New York: HarperCollins, 2005.

Taylor-Butler, Christine. *Mercury*. New York: Scholastic, 2005.

Vogt, Gregory. *Solar System*. New York: Scholastic, 2001.

Explore the Web

Enchanted Learning: Mercury http://www.zoomschool.com/subjects/ astronomy/planets/mercury

Funschool: Space http://funschool.kaboose.com/globe-rider/space/ index.html?trnstl=1

StarChild: The Planet Mercury http://starchild.gsfc.nasa.gov/docs/StarChild/ solar_system_level1/mercury.html